WHEN THE GAME IS OVER

IT ALL GOES

BACK IN THE

PARTICIPANT'S GUIDE

Resources by John Ortberg

An Ordinary Day with Jesus
(curriculum with Ruth Haley Barton)

Everybody's Normal Till You Get to Know Them
(book, audio)

God Is Closer Than You Think
(book, audio, curriculum with Stephen and Amanda Sorenson)

If You Want to Walk on Water, You've Got to Get Out of the Boat
(book, audio, curriculum with Stephen and Amanda Sorenson)

The Life You've Always Wanted
(book, audio, curriculum with Stephen and Amanda Sorenson)

Living the God Life

Love Beyond Reason

Old Testament Challenge
(curriculum series with Kevin and Sherry Harney)

When the Game Is Over, It All Goes Back in the Box
(book, audio, curriculum with Stephen and Amanda Sorenson)

JOHN ORTBERG

WITH STEPHEN AND AMANDA SORENSON

WHEN THE GAME IS OVER

IT ALL GOES

BACK IN THE

PARTICIPANT'S GUIDE

SIX SESSIONS ON LIVING LIFE
IN LIGHT OF ETERNITY

ZONDERVAN.com/
AUTHORTRACKER
follow your favorite authors

We want to hear from you. Please send your comments about this book to us in care of zreview@zondervan.com. Thank you.

ZONDERVAN®

When the Game Is Over, It All Goes Back in the Box Participant's Guide
Copyright © 2008 by John Ortberg

Requests for information should be addressed to:

Zondervan, *Grand Rapids, Michigan 49530*

ISBN 978-0-310-28246-4

Interior design by Beth Shagene

Printed in the United States of America

09 10 11 12 13 14 • 23 22 21 20 19 18 17 16 15 14 13 12 11 10 9 8 7 6

CONTENTS

SESSION 1

When the Game Is Over, It All Goes Back in the Box 7

SESSION 2

Keeping Score Where It Really Counts 23

SESSION 3

Resign as Master of the Board 39

SESSION 4

Calling or Comfort? Choose Your Moves Wisely 57

SESSION 5

Playing the Game with Greatness and Grace 75

SESSION 6

The King Has One More Move. 91

WHEN THE GAME IS OVER, IT ALL GOES BACK IN THE BOX

Life, no matter how we play it, will not go on forever.
When the game is over it's all going to end up in the same place.
As an ancient Italian proverb put it: "Pawn and king alike,
they all go back in the bag."

JOHN ORTBERG

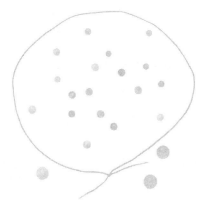

Let's Think About It (3 minutes)

Imagine for a moment that life is like a game.

What, then, is our goal or objective — what is it that we want to "win" in the game of life?

What do you think is the most important secret to learn in order to play the game of life well?

DVD Observations (20 minutes)

As you watch this session's teaching segment, feel free to use the following outline as a guide for taking notes.

Learning to play the game

When the game is over

Learning to number our days

Learning to be rich toward God

DVD Discussion (5 minutes)

1. What is the great lesson of life that John learned through playing Monopoly®, and why is it such an important lesson to learn?

When have you wished, as John did when he finally beat his grandmother at Monopoly, that your accomplishments could remain as a permanent memorial of your greatness? What did you learn as a result of that unmet desire?

✓ 2. Which attitudes and actions often become evident in our lives when we lose sight of the everything-goes-back-in-the-box truth? *use people   love things*

Which of your personal experiences or observations of other people and their experiences stand out in your mind as reminders of the truth that everything goes back in the box?

3. How would you define what it means to be "rich toward God"? What might a life that is rich toward God look like?

Bible Exploration (18 minutes)

1. Read Luke 12:13 – 21 (Jesus' story of the rich fool), then discuss which images stand out to you — and why.

What are some ways in which people today demonstrate the attitudes and actions of the brothers or the rich fool in Jesus' story?

How does Jesus' response to the man's question about sharing in his brother's inheritance cause you to want to reorder your life priorities?

2. The Bible has much to say about the nature and meaning of life and how to live it well. Let's consider a few representative passages to see how its perspective differs from ours.

a. What is the source of everything we are and everything we have in life? (See Deuteronomy 8:17–18; Psalm 24:1; James 1:17.) In what ways does this contradict our human-centered perspective?

b. Although we may want our accomplishments to last forever, what does the Bible say happens to them when our life is over? (See Job 1:21; Ecclesiastes 2:18–23; 1 John 2:15–17.)

c. In contrast to the belief that achievement brings contentment, what is the "secret" to being truly content in life? (See Matthew 6:19–20; 1 Timothy 6:6–8; Hebrews 13:5.) What are some ways we can put the biblical principles of contentment into practice in our daily lives?

Just a Reminder ...

What lasts forever?	What goes back in the box?
God	Possessions, money, and pleasures
Other people	My résumé, titles, and positions
My soul	My body, physical attractiveness, youth, and health
Deeds of love	Power and security People's opinions of me

DVD Wrap-up (3 minutes)

As you watch this final DVD clip, feel free to jot down notes or questions.

Personal Journey:
To Do Now (5 minutes)

All of us have hopes and dreams for life. We long to play the game to win, but often the life we want seems to slip from our grasp. We lose sight of what is truly important and expend our energy on things that merely go back in the box when the game is over. That's why the message of Psalm 90:12 is so important for us to take to heart: "Teach us to number our days aright, that we may gain a heart of wisdom."

1. As you consider your life — where you have been, where you are today, where you'd like to be (and what you'd like to do) tomorrow — what is it you are trying to "win" and which strategy are you using in the game?

   Do you think your goal and strategy will truly satisfy you? Why or why not?

2. What impact has this session had on your perspective of what is *temporary* and *eternal*?

Which perspective, the temporal or the eternal, has most influenced your everyday decisions in the past? If you need to develop a more eternal perspective, how might you go about doing that?

3. To what extent have you been seeking to live a life that is rich in God's eyes? How might you want this to change in the future?

4. Throughout the Bible, God makes it clear that he desires to be in relationship with the people he has created — to "be their God" and to "dwell among them" (Exodus 29:45–46). So, if we want to live a life that is rich toward God, the most important thing is to give him the full devotion of our hearts. Perhaps this desire is best expressed in a conversation that took place between Jesus and Peter in John 21:15–17:

> When they had finished eating, Jesus said to Simon Peter, "Simon son of John, do you truly love me more than these?"
> "Yes, Lord," he said, "you know that I love you."
> Jesus said, "Feed my lambs."

Again Jesus said, "Simon son of John, do you truly love me?"

He answered, "Yes, Lord, you know that I love you."

Jesus said, "Take care of my sheep."

The third time he said to him, "Simon son of John, do you love me?"

Peter was hurt because Jesus asked him the third time, "Do you love me?" He said, "Lord, you know all things; you know that I love you."

Jesus said, "Feed my sheep."

The devotion that Jesus was asking of Peter was the devotion of loving God with all of his heart, soul, mind, and strength and then loving people as he loved himself. It's an opportunity God still offers to people today: "If anyone loves me, he will obey my teaching. My Father will love him, and we will come to him and make our home with him" (John 14:23). How will you respond?

> *I can't make myself love God, but I can come to know him better.*
> *I can choose to be with him. I learn to see his goodness in creation*
> *and beauty. I take time to ask for his help as we work together. I see*
> *him in the people with whom I meet. I hear his voice in what I read.*
> *I ask his forgiveness for the many times I mess up. I thank him at*
> *the end of the day for his presence in it. I can spend this day loving*
> *God. And tomorrow I can seek to love him a little more.*
> *This is a life "rich toward God."*
> **JOHN ORTBERG**

Personal Journey: To Do on Your Own

Despite all of the materialistic influences surrounding us, we can learn to focus more on the *eternal* than the *temporary*. In fact, there's no better time than right now to begin living out the truth that "it all goes back in the box."

1. During the next few days, think about how much time and energy you devote to things in your life that are temporary and how much time and energy you devote to things that are eternal. Then write down any changes you want to make in light of what you discover.

Which specific changes will you make during the next week, the next two weeks, the next month to increasingly build your life around what is eternal rather than what is temporary?

2. In Luke 12:21, Jesus urged people to be "rich toward God." But how do we go about doing this in everyday life? The verses listed on page 20 will give you some direction in how to be rich toward God. It is up to you to identify and start taking the steps that will focus your life around eternal things that really matter. After reading each passage, identify the appropriate general principle for being rich toward God, then write down a specific, practical step you will take to start living out that principle in your life. Then start taking those steps!

Ways I can choose to be rich toward God	Specific steps I will take to build a life that is rich toward God
Deuteronomy 10:12	
Nehemiah 9:5b – 6	
Psalm 25:4 – 5; 119:111	
Psalm 82:3 – 4	
John 10:27	
John 13:34 – 35	
1 Timothy 6:18	
1 Peter 2:21; 1 John 2:3 – 6	
1 Peter 4:10	

What It Means to Be Rich toward God

In his book, *When the Game Is Over, It All Goes Back in the Box*, John Ortberg wrote:

- Being rich toward God means growing a soul that is increasingly healthy and good.
- Being rich toward God means loving and enjoying the people around you.
- Being rich toward God means learning about your gifts and passions and doing good work to help improve the world.
- Being rich toward God means becoming generous with your stuff.
- Being rich toward God means that which is *temporary* becomes the servant of that which is *eternal*.
- Being rich toward God means savoring every roll of the dice and every trip around the board.

Read these maxims every day, and determine which of them you are willing to apply. Then start doing it.

Wise people, build Their lives Around whot is eTernal + Squeeze in whaT is Temporary

KEEPING SCORE WHERE IT REALLY COUNTS

We are, by nature, scorekeepers. We crave feedback.
We want to know how we're doing. Keeping score is really about
defining reality. It's the way we determine what counts
and what doesn't count. To talk about how we keep score
is really to talk about how we define success.

JOHN ORTBERG

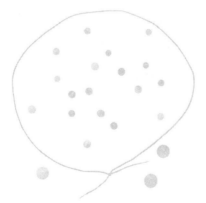

Let's Think About It (3 minutes)

There are many different ways to define "success." Take a few minutes to identify some of the ways we define success vocationally, financially, socially, intellectually, physically, and spiritually. Then talk about the standards by which we measure success in each of these areas.

DVD Observations (20 minutes)

As you watch this session's teaching segment, feel free to use the following outline as a guide for taking notes.

We are all scorekeepers

How we learn to keep score
    Comparing

    Competing

    Climbing the ladder

Playing to win the *inner* game

DVD Discussion (5 minutes)

1. How do we learn to keep score — to know what counts and what doesn't — and what are we trying to accomplish when we keep score?

2. In the video, John Ortberg identifies the three "Cs" of keeping score: comparison, competition, and climbing the ladder.

   a. What impact do you think comparing ourselves to other people has on our state of contentment?

   b. What are some of the consequences we face personally and in our relationships with others when keeping score through competition becomes toxic?

c. If we're ladder climbers, what happens to our scoring system when we realize that Jesus not only didn't grasp for equality with God but actually climbed *down* the ladder to be a sacrifice and servant for all?

3. Our culture values the *outer you* so highly that it's easy for us to overlook and neglect the *inner you*. Although we may nod our heads and agree that we need to pay more attention to the inner you, it's not easy to do. What kinds of things nurture the inner you, and what hinders us from actually doing these things—from playing the game that counts forever?

Bible Exploration (18 minutes)

1. People have been keeping score since the beginning of history. As you read the following passages that reveal how different people in the Bible kept score, consider: (1) the consequences that keeping score can have on our relationships with people, our relationship with God, and God's work in the world, and (2) how keeping score in these situations affected both the outer and inner you.

Bible passage	Relational impact	Impact on the inner/ outer you
Genesis 4:1–16	Cain	out from the Lords Presence 16
1 Samuel 18:5–16	David & Saul	Lord had left him v.12
Esther 5:7–14	Mordecai Haman	
Philippians 1:12–26		Get ahead

2. There is a huge difference between the scoring system for the outer game by which most of us measure our success and God's scoring system for the inner game — the game that really counts. As you read the Bible passages below and on page 30, identify the guiding principles of God's scoring system and then discuss what these contrasting scoring systems reveal about society's and God's definitions of success.

Society's scoring system for the outer you	God's scoring system for the inner you
Get ahead at all costs, even if it pushes a few people back	See Mark 10:42–45
Climb the ladder of success	See Isaiah 2:12; 1 Timothy 6:10–11
Compete to show how much better you are than others	See Psalm 49:16–17

Society's scoring system for the outer you	God's scoring system for the inner you
Get everything you can now	See John 6:27
What we have, what we do, and how others view us reveal our worth	See Luke 12:7; Philippians 3:7-9; 1 John 3:1
Earthly rewards are all that matter	See 1 Corinthians 3:12-15; Ephesians 6:8

3. When we compete, compare, and ladder climb in order to achieve the best that can be won for the benefit of our outer you, what are the consequences to our inner you? (See Ecclesiastes 4:4; Galatians 6:8; James 3:16.)

4. How can we learn the secrets to winning the inner game of life, the game that really counts? (See Psalm 25:4–5, 8–10.)

DVD Wrap-up (3 minutes)

As you watch this final DVD clip, feel free to jot down notes or questions.

Right After DVD

Personal Journey:
To Do Now (5 minutes)

We are, by nature, scorekeepers. We commonly gauge our success in life by the three "Cs": comparing ourselves to people, competing with people, and climbing up the ladder.

1. Think about your life from childhood until now.

   a. Who taught you the most about how to keep score?

b. Which were the most important lessons you learned about keeping score?

c. By which standards are you keeping score—evaluating your success in life—right now?

d. To what extent are you satisfied or dissatisfied with: the way you define success? the scorekeeping system you are using?

2. We each have a choice regarding the game — the *inner* game or *outer* game — to which we will devote our energy and time. Which game consumes the most time and energy in your life, and is that the way you want to live? Why or why not?

3. Consider one practical thing you can start doing today to invest more heavily in the inner you that will last for eternity.

> *Be grateful for the outer you. Come to peace with your body.*
> *Rejoice in its strengths. Accept it in its limitations.*
> *Be grateful for it. Wash it every once in a while. Let it work hard.*
> *Be happy when it gets promoted. But remember, it's wasting away.*
> *The inner you, on the other hand, is capable of a glory*
> *that right now you cannot even imagine.*
>
> **JOHN ORTBERG**

Personal Journey: To Do on Your Own

No matter how much we may want to invest in the inner you—the part of us that God values most highly—it isn't easy. Every day, we will have to fight the urge to make the outer you most important. The challenges of daily life will continually pull our focus from that which lasts forever to the tyranny of the here and now.

1. While Jesus was here on earth he provided a living example of how to remain focused on what was most important, despite the pressures and challenges of daily life. What do you learn about mastering the inner game from the following glimpses into Jesus' life?

   a. John 4:34; 6:38

   b. John 13:12–17; Philippians 2:5–11

c. Matthew 14:23; Luke 4:42 – 44; 11:1 – 4

2. If you truly want to shift your focus from success for the *outer you* to investing in the *inner you*, you will have to make some changes. Try doing each of the following things for the next five days.

- **Spend time with God (Psalm 16:7 – 11)**
  Set aside time each day to be quiet before God so that you may learn from him. Share with him your hopes, your struggles, and your desire to invest your life in what really counts. (See Psalm 119:10 – 16.)

- **Focus your thoughts on what is eternal (2 Corinthians 4:18)**
  Ask God to focus your thoughts on what is most important — not just in this life, but in the next. (See Philippians 3:9, 20 – 21.)

- **Confess your sins to God (1 John 1:8 – 9)**
  Ask him to purify your motives and to help you make choices that bring you closer to him. (See Psalm 139:23 – 24.)

- **Put your faith into action (1 Timothy 6:17 – 19)**
  Review your calendar and checkbook, your attitudes and your thought life. Where are your priorities, *really*? (See Colossians 3:23 – 24.)

Measuring Tools for the Inner You

Mirrors, scales, cameras, yardsticks—all of these help us track the progress of the outer you, but which tools help us track the progress of the inner you? Consider the following:

- Self-examination of heart and thought life, calendar and checkbook
- Commitment to discover and obey the Word of God
- Friends who love you enough to speak the truth to you
- Time to be alone with and listen to God for the renewal of the inner you

RESIGN AS MASTER OF THE BOARD

If I have surrendered, if I have put God in control,
then I can release all outcomes.... I don't have to carry the weight
of the world anymore. I can be open to face each day
with a sense of wonder, gratitude, freedom, relaxation, and delight
because God — not me — is now the Master of the Board.

JOHN ORTBERG

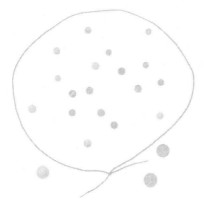

Let's Think About It (3 minutes)

It's human nature to try to be "Master of the Board," to be able to exercise at least some degree of control over our lives, to acquire something that is ours and ours alone.

What do you think we are trying to gain, and what benefits do we hope to receive, when we seek to control our lives?

Human nature

why do we Try To be Master of the board —

How much of our lives do we control, *really*?

DVD Observations (20 minutes)

As you watch this session's teaching segment, feel free to use the following outline as a guide for taking notes.

The illusion that our stuff is really ours

The freedom of resigning as Master of the Board

The truth about the stuff we treasure *How much is enough?*
More will never be enough

Choose your treasure carefully

DVD Discussion (5 minutes)

1. How important to us is the illusion that we are in control of our lives, and why is it so important that we maintain that illusion?

   What are we willing to sacrifice in order to maintain the illusion of control?   Control Freak

2. What do we gain when we choose to resign as Master of the Board—when we say "yes!" to God and surrender control of our lives to him?

3. How would you describe the differences between the *richness of having* and the *richness of being?*

Although we are inclined to think of richness as being a result of acquisition, how does giving stuff away to benefit the kingdom of God make us rich in being?

Bible Exploration (17 minutes)

1. We like to think that we are in control, that when it comes to our own life and destiny we are the Master of the Board. But as it often does, the Bible opens our eyes to a different perspective. It exposes the truth we rarely want to face: there is an ultimate Master of the Board — and we are not it.

   As you consider the Bible passages on page 44 that show God to be the master over all earthly things, discuss how his control over the earth and everything in it affects our daily lives. For example, although we make plans for the future as if we control it, our very existence is not up to us at all — it's a gift from God.

we need reminded

Bible passage	Who is really in control of what?	What does this mean we don't control?
1 Chronicles 29:11–12		
Psalm 24:1		
Psalm 33:10–11, 16–19		
Proverbs 19:21		
Acts 17:24–28		

2. The Bible includes the stories of many people who lived as if they were the Master of the Board rather than acknowledging God as Master of the Board. Two of these stories are about kings, who admittedly were masters of much more than most of us could ever hope to be. Notice what happened when they refused to live in obedience to the Master of the Board and pursued life as if they were in control. Who proved to be the ultimate Master of the Board? (See 2 Chronicles 26:3–5, 16–21; Daniel 4:28–35.)

3. In contrast to kings Uzziah and Nebuchadnezzar, King David understood who was Master of the Board; his confidence rested securely in God's goodness as Lord and Master of all. Read David's prayer in 1 Chronicles 29:10–18 and note the various ways he expresses God's ultimate authority.

Can you see yourself responding to God in the same way? Why or why not?

DVD Wrap-up (3 minutes)

As you watch this final DVD clip, feel free to jot down notes or questions.

Examples - where Gods leading proved To be - far beyond what you could have imagined -

Personal Journey:
To Do Now (5 minutes)

We long to be Master of the Board. We'll do almost anything to hold onto the illusion that we have acquired the riches we want and have life under control. We clutter our lives with stuff: people, events, possessions—all to bolster the illusion. But we come up empty because what we really long for is the richness of *being*, not the richness of *having*.

> *It's not bad to play the game.*
> *It's not bad to be really good at it.*
> *It's not bad to be the Master of the Board....*
> *But there are always more rungs to climb,*
> *more money to be made, more deals to pull off.*
> **JOHN ORTBERG**

1. Before the Israelites entered the Promised Land, Moses gave them a strong warning to never lose sight of who is Master of the Board. (See Deuteronomy 6:10–12; 8:10–20.)

   a. Why was this warning important to Israel?

b. What does this warning say to you about the danger of having riches and therefore assuming that you are Master of the Board?

2. When you operate as if you are Master of the Board and create the illusion that you can successfully control outcomes and "engineer" life, what results in terms of your view of yourself and your work? What about your attitudes toward life, God, and other people?

When you are intent on being Master of the Board, which wonderful surprises might you be missing?

Which of God's blessings might you be taking for granted, thinking that they come from your efforts and the "control" you exert?

The process of surrendering

3. In the book on which this curriculum is based, John Ortberg observed, "Only if one experiences that God is good is it possible to surrender to him unconditionally one's whole heart, soul, and being." How does your view of God (what you believe about his trustworthiness, competency, and love for you, for example) influence your ability and willingness to surrender all aspects of your life to him—and allow him to be Master of the Board?

Personal Journey: To Do on Your Own

1. In the book *When the Game Is Over, It All Goes Back in the Box*, John Ortberg says of our human condition: "The reality of this world is that I was born into Someone Else's kingdom. My life came to me as a gift I did not choose; it is suspended from a slender thread that I did not weave and cannot on my own sustain." To what extent are you living out this truth, and to what extent are you living in the illusion that you control your life?

What changes might you expect to see in your life if you were to resign as Master of the Board and start living out this truth?

What may be hindering you from surrendering your life — your gifts, energies, resources, "stuff," and heart — to God as Master of the Board?

2. Although releasing our grip on the controls of life may seem like it will end life as we know it (which, in a sense, it does), what did Jesus teach will happen when we freely yield our little centers of control to God? (See Matthew 16:24–27; John 12:24.)

What evidences have you seen of God bringing to fruition something new and wonderful after you have given him complete control?

3. When we surrender our lives to God and allow him to be the ultimate Master of the Board, we open up our lives to receive priceless blessings. What are some of these blessings, and what would it mean to you to receive them?

Psalm 119:161 – 165

Proverbs 3:5 – 6

Isaiah 40:31

Matthew 6:25 – 33; 7:9 – 12

Galatians 5:22 – 23

Philippians 4:6 – 7

1 John 1:9

4. Once we accept the reality that God is in control and surrender control of our life to him as the rightful Master of the
Board, we will need to make some adjustments as we learn to
live in a way that is rich toward God. The process outlined
below can help you get started. (The chart on pages 53 – 54
provides an example as well as space for your thoughts.)

- Set aside some time to reflect specifically on what in life is
  important to you — your dreams, attitudes toward money,
  motivation, relationships, use of time, anxieties, hopes,
  desire to acquire stuff, etc.

- Consider each area of importance and ask yourself to
  what extent you trust God with this part of your life.

- Ask God to reveal any area(s) in which you are holding
  on to control and not trusting him. Confess your lack of
  trust to God and ask him to help you let go and trust him
  to be Master of the Board.

- Then identify specific steps of trust you can take that will
  demonstrate in thought, attitude, and action that you are
  giving God ultimate control of your life. For example, if
  ambition is one way you have been trying to be Master
  of the Board, you may need to examine and change
  your attitude toward your coworkers and begin loving
  them as Christ loves them rather than viewing them as
  "competition" for the goals you desire to achieve.

What in life is important to me?	To what extent do I trust God in this area?	Steps of trust I can take to let God be Master of the Board
EXAMPLE: I want a secure retirement	Maybe not too much — I'm more consistent in my 401(k) contributions than in my giving	I can remind myself frequently of how God promises to provide for those who love him; I can change my giving habits — maybe even have an accountability partner; I can start giving of my time now — that's something I want to do when I retire

What in life is important to me?	To what extent do I trust God in this area?	Steps of trust I can take to let God be Master of the Board

I sometimes wonder how our sense of control looks to God because we think that stuff is ours. We think that our lives are ours. That our minds are ours ... that I'm in control — I'm smart enough, strong enough, clever enough. I can run my own life. The reality is, I can't even run my own heartbeat.

JOHN ORTBERG

CALLING OR COMFORT? CHOOSE YOUR MOVES WISELY

If there is a challenge in front of you, a course of action
that would cause you to grow and that would be helpful
to people around you, but you find yourself scared about it,
there's a real good chance that God is in that challenge....
If you're not facing any challenges too big for you,
if it has been a while since you have felt scared, there's a real
good chance that you've been sitting in the chair too long.

JOHN ORTBERG

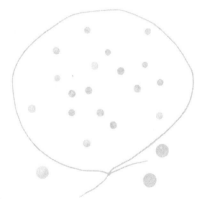

Let's Think About It (3 minutes)

When it comes to playing the game of life, we can choose to relax and play it safe in the comfort of an "EZ" chair, or we can go after our calling and accept whatever risks accompany the challenge.

✓ No matter which we choose—the comfort of the chair or the risk of the calling—we will eventually arrive at the end of the game. But what, in your opinion, are the price and the prize of each option?

DVD Observations (19 minutes)

As you watch this session's teaching segment, feel free to use the following outline as a guide for taking notes.

The most dangerous chair in the house

You can't just sit there

God never calls with an easy assignment

You were made for a mission

DVD Discussion (5 minutes)

1. Why is the EZ chair the most dangerous object in the house?

What has been your experience with getting *too* comfortable in life, and how has it affected which moves you take in the game?

2. What kind of "assignments" does God call people to do?

Why are we inclined (at least initially) to say "no" to God when he extends a call to us?

What encourages us to say "yes" to him?

3. As you heard the story of "Johnny the bagger," what did you think and feel?

What has Johnny the bagger learned about life, calling, and choosing the next move that you can apply to your own life?

Sometimes people think they are robbed of any chance at having a significant mission in life because of their weaknesses. In fact, the opposite is true. God never wastes a hurt. Part of what makes a human life more powerful is the struggle.

JOHN ORTBERG

Bible Exploration (18 minutes)

We take a "turn" at life every time we make a choice—what we will eat, who we will spend time with, how much we will give, what we will do after work. No one else can take our turn. There are no designated hitters. We are not allowed to "pass." Our life becomes the sum of all of the choices we make, so we ought to choose our next moves wisely.

1. Daniel stands out as a champion of making wise choices at each roll of the dice. Even in the midst of life-threatening challenges, he flourished because he refused to believe he was helpless. Confident that God was with him, he took the risks to live out his deepest commitments and to follow God's call at every turn.

   a. What does Daniel 1:1–7 reveal about Daniel's circumstances? How would you rate his chances of being in a position to live out God's calling on his life?

   b. According to Daniel 1:8–14, what strategic move did Daniel make in order to reclaim his ability to live according to God's call?

c. After Daniel made his move in faith, what did God cause
to happen? (See Daniel 1:15–20.) What had Daniel
gained that taking a turn in the EZ chair would not have
accomplished?

d. One of the remarkable qualities of Daniel's character is
that he never stopped playing the game to win. After he
had been granted high status in the kingdom of Persia,
what risky move did Daniel choose (Daniel 6:1–11), and
what was the result (6:12–23)?

2. From this brief glimpse into Daniel's choices to accept the risk
of God's calling, what have you learned about:

a. The kinds of assignments God gives?

b. How the next big move on the board may present itself?

c. What is at stake when you choose your next move?

3. When God calls someone to accomplish a mission, the task
   is almost always bigger than anything the person can imagine
   doing, so accepting the call is a bold move that represents a
   giant step of faith. But God doesn't call us to take our moves
   alone in our own strength; he reassures us that he will be with
   us every step of the way. What encouragement do the following Bible passages provide, and how does each passage help
   you to accept the challenge of taking bold steps of faith?

   Psalm 9:10

   Psalm 27:1–3

Psalm 37:23 – 24

Psalm 55:22

Psalm 56:3 – 4

Romans 8:35 – 39

> *What really matters when God calls you to do something*
> *is not whether or not you feel inadequate.*
> *Of course you will; you are inadequate. So am I.*
> *That's why God promises to go with us.*
> *What matters is your decision. Only people who say yes*
> *to challenge, demand, and risk are ever fully alive.*
> **JOHN ORTBERG**

DVD Wrap-up (3 minutes)

As you watch this final DVD clip, feel free to jot down notes or questions.

Personal Journey:
To Do Now (5 minutes)

How aware are you of how you are filling the "squares" of your life? After taking a moment to consider what fills your days, shade in the portion of the square below that is consumed by the busy "things" of life, leaving open the part that is available for God's calling on your life. Then answer the related questions on pages 67–68.

1. You were made for a mission—a calling. What is yours? How well is it represented on your square?

2. If you haven't discovered your calling yet, what steps can you take to develop a keener sense of God's presence in your life and become more attentive to listening for his calling?

   Who knows you well enough to help you identify what God is calling you to do and loves you enough to challenge you when you want to shrink back from God's mission? Be sure to include that person in the process. Invite him or her to pray with you and to hold you accountable as you seek to discover and respond to God's calling.

3. Now start making your personal list of what you want to remove from your square and what you want to include in your square. Then begin, one item at a time, to roll the dice and make your move. Play the game to win!

The things I want out of my square	The calling I want to fill my square

Personal Journey: To Do on Your Own

According to John Ortberg, "God has given you a tiny measure of what he has without limit—the ability to choose." We can choose what to get rid of in our lives. We can choose what to do with our lives. We can choose how to order our days. We can choose to make changes that will enable us to live out the calling God has given us, but first we need to identify the obstacles that stand in our way.

1. In his book, John Ortberg talks about "shadow missions," substitute games we were not meant to play. What are the main shadow missions that you gravitate toward and try to win when you allow your natural temptations and selfishness to take over?

2. What do you think are the biggest obstacles keeping you from "rolling the dice" and stepping out in faith to answer God's call?

To what extent are you so comfortable that you don't want to take on the challenges of the game?

What are your fears related to the challenges God has given you, and in what ways are they holding you back?

To what extent does busyness crowd out what you would consider to be the most important things in life?

3. Choosing how we spend our time goes a long way toward determining what ends up in our "square." In his book, John Ortberg suggests looking at life using the following categories of activities in which we must engage to pursue life for God's kingdom. Set aside time to do a careful inventory of how you spend your time in each category, review what you discover, then create a revised time inventory that will more accurately reflect what you want to put in your "square."

Category	How I spend my time	How I want to spend my time
Have-tos — things you must do: sleeping, eating, etc.		
God — studying Bible, praying, etc.		
People — serving family, friends, coworkers, neighbors, the poor and hurting, etc.		
Calling — your mission from God; developing gifts he has given you		
Joy — being a joy sharer who counts blessings		

In his book, John Ortberg also offers this challenge:

During the next ten days, pick an area where you can take action. And choose to honor God in that area.... Perhaps for the next ten days, what will help you take your turn is to become intensely aware of all the decisions that are open to you. Some are small ... what you wear, how you comb your hair, what you read, what you listen to, who you call on the phone, what route you take to work. Some decisions will be larger, such as refusing to allow your boss or spouse the power to dictate what kind of mood you will be in during the day based on how he or she treats you.

Never give up your spirit. Never yield emotionally. Take action, and find meaning in suffering.

When you resolve in your heart to honor God, he becomes involved in your life in ways you cannot forsee.

It's your turn now.

Your "Signature Strengths"

In his book, *When the Game Is Over, It All Goes Back in the Box*, John Ortberg shares Martin Seligman's "signature strengths," which we each can use to seek the good life. But John recognizes that "the best life — the meaningful life, being on mission — is when we use our signature strengths in the service of something larger than ourselves." Think about which of these strengths best fit you and how you are using them:

- Wisdom and knowledge (which include abilities like curiosity, love of learning, judgment, and social intelligence)
- Courage (perseverance and integrity)
- Humanity (with capacities for kindness)
- Justice (the ability to bring about fairness and leadership)
- Temperance (qualities like self-control, prudence, humility)
- Transcendence (the appreciation of beauty, the expression of gratitude, the ability to hope, the capacity for joy)

PLAYING THE GAME WITH GREATNESS AND GRACE

The number-one rule if you want to win, to compete, is,
be the kind of person other people want to sit next to.
And the Bible's word for that is *grace*.
We have to learn how to live, how to play the game with grace.

JOHN ORTBERG

Let's Think About It (3 minutes)

We all feel the thrill when we see competitive greatness in action. What are some of the characteristics of competitive greatness, and what do these qualities inspire in us when we see them exhibited in others?

DVD Observations (16 minutes)

As you watch this session's teaching segment, feel free to use the following outline as a guide for taking notes.

The fire of competitive greatness

Quitter or competitor?

Winning is something we do together

Playing the game with grace

DVD Discussion (5 minutes)

1. What did you feel as John described the great race between Sea Biscuit and War Admiral?

   Which other great competitions — personal, spiritual, athletic, academic, or political — did it bring to mind?

2. Some things can hinder us from running a strong spiritual race while other things encourage us to continue strong in our faith. Which things tend to demotivate us and lead us to quit and choose easier paths?

   Which things tend to inspire us and help turn a potential quitter into a committed competitor?

3. John Ortberg said, "Winning and staying gracious is one of the great tests of character because now I have to remember that winning is not all about me." Many of us need help in learning both how to win and lose with grace.

   a. If you were to teach a seminar on winning with grace, which key points would you emphasize?

   b. If you were to teach a seminar on losing with grace, which key points would you include?

> *There is something about drive, the competitive quest for greatness, about the search for mastery and striving for excellence that moves us really deeply. The real contest is to see if I can offer my best, to see if I can run and not give up in the face of a great demand.*
> **JOHN ORTBERG**

Bible Exploration (19 minutes)

1. When we entrust our hearts and lives to God, believing that he loves and cares for us, we sometimes expect that our lives will not be painful or difficult. But God desires something far more important than comfort for those who follow him.

   a. What do we learn from the following Bible passages about how God cares for us in the midst of difficulty and trials? (See Psalm 37:39–40; Matthew 6:34; Philippians 4:6–7.)

   b. What can the challenges and suffering of life produce in us? (See Romans 5:1–5; 2 Corinthians 1:3–11; 2 Timothy 2:3; 4:5; James 1:2–4; 1 Peter 1:3–9.)

   What role do these qualities play in helping us run the race with greatness and grace?

2. Competitive greatness arises from a love for the battle, a resolve that welcomes the opportunity to do our best when our best is required. The competitive drive of a runner to win the race was one of the apostle Paul's favorite images of the life of faith. Let's see how the following descriptive images can help us learn how to compete well.

   a. What is the goal of competing, and how must one prepare to compete well? (See 1 Corinthians 9:24 – 27.)

   What are some of the ways we can apply these images to our lives, particularly our spiritual lives?

   b. What must we do in order to compete well during the race? (See Philippians 3:13 – 14; Hebrews 12:1 – 3.)

How hard is it to compete well during the race?

What practical ideas can you share with the group regarding how to run the race well when we face fatigue, pressure, conflict, or difficulties?

c. What satisfaction will we find in running the race well, and what will be our reward? (See 2 Timothy 4:7–8.)

DVD Wrap-up (3 minutes)

As you watch this final DVD clip, feel free to jot down notes or questions. There is also space provided to complete the exercise John Ortberg describes in the video.

_____

_____ - _____?_____

What will you do with your "dash"?

Personal Journey:
To Do Now (5 minutes)

So, what have you been doing with your "dash" so far? How might you want to adjust it from here on? It's yours to spend any way you see fit. The race is on.

1. The apostle Paul used athletic metaphors to describe his dash — "straining toward what is ahead," "fight the good fight," "kept the faith," etc. Which metaphors would describe how you have conducted your dash?

2. Consider some of your accomplishments that reflect how you have run the race.

   a. To what extent have you run with determination, heart, and courage when you have been under pressure?

   b. In what ways have you grown because you refused to quit when things became difficult?

c. To what extent have you "opted out" when challenges surfaced?

d. What would people who know you the best say about your response to difficulties?

e. Which things may be holding you back from running a great race?

f. How committed are you to strict training so that you can run with greatness and grace?

3. What are you "running" to obtain—an earthly prize? an eternal prize? How does the prize you hope to receive influence the moves you make as you play the game?

> There is a score inside us, a measure of determination
> and heart and courage under pressure that matters
> more than the points on the board. Winning and losing apart
> from this inner score do not matter much.
>
> **JOHN ORTBERG**

Personal Journey: To Do on Your Own

In Monopoly, winning takes cooperation—trades and deals. So one of the keys to playing the game well is to be the kind of person others want to sit next to. Nobody likes a whining, disgruntled loser, and nobody likes to lose to a gloating know-it-all.

1. Not surprisingly, the Bible has much to say about being the kind of person other people want to sit next to. The Bible's word for this is *grace*. Those who play the game well play it with grace. Each of the Bible passages on page 87 offers sage advice for living life with grace. As you read them, make sure you understand the advice they offer, then think about how you can do a better job of playing the game with grace.

Bible passage	Advice for living with grace	What I need to do to play the game with more grace
Proverbs 13:10	Humble	
Romans 12:16–18	Live peacefully with others	
1 Corinthians 13:4–5	Love wins Proude rude	
Galatians 5:26	don't become conceited	
Ephesians 4:31–32	Get Rid of bitterness Rage malice	
Philippians 2:14–15	don't complain + dispute	
Philippians 4:8	Think on best Things Thought Life	
Colossians 3:8–10	dirty TALK	
Colossians 4:6	Conversation Full of Grace	
James 1:19	slow to Anger	

2. On a scale of one to ten (ten being high), how gracious do you consider yourself to be at:

Winning?

Losing?

Forgiving people who wrong you?

3. How often do people want to "sit" next to you as you play the game? Are you willing to ask God to reveal your sins and faults to you so that, with his help, you can become a competitor who demonstrates grace? (If not, why not? Be honest!)

4. The apostle Paul wrote, "Do nothing out of selfish ambition or vain conceit ... look not only to your own interests, but also to the interests of others" (Philippians 2:3 – 4). Or, as John Ortberg has discovered, "The way the real game is played, our most cherished and meaningful wins come when we are helping someone else." Are you playing the game this way? The people factor adds eternal value to the outcome of the game.

The people in your game	Ways I can play the game to benefit and bring out the best in people
Family members	
Long-time friends	
Acquaintances	
Coworkers	
Neighbors	
Schoolmates	
Others:	

At the cross we see what grace looks like when it loses, when it wins, when it forgives. And people are still hoping to sit next to someone who looks like that.
JOHN ORTBERG

THE KING HAS ONE MORE MOVE

There is a kind of trophy that will wear out.
It'll go back in the box.
But there's another trophy that will last through all eternity,
and that is to delight the heart of God.

JOHN ORTBERG

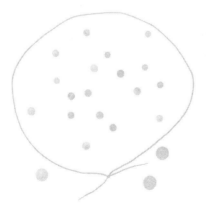

Let's Think About It (3 minutes)

When we play a game, we play to receive some kind of reward—perhaps recognition, a prize, or a trophy. So what kinds of "trophies" do people pursue in the game of life?

DVD Observations (13 minutes)

As you watch this session's teaching segment, feel free to use the following outline as a guide for taking notes.

Playing for trophies

Sooner or later, the game ends

iS mo old

30 yr old

96 yr

dash denying

if A man has nothing he's willing To die for

he's not fit for piving

— Thats ALL folks — most live

— Believe in me will never die

The hope for something more —

-The King has one more move — in you life — no

Matter where you find yourself

May be A pawn or A King still has one more move

No rewind Button

DVD Discussion (6 minutes)

1. After a while, living for trophies can become a hollow pursuit. What happens to most of the trophies we pursue, and why?

   Which trophies are worth playing for, and why?

2. No matter how much we want to deny it, the game of life will one day come to an end. When that day comes, what happens to all the "stuff" we've won during the game?

   When the game comes to an end, what really matters about how you have been playing the game?

3. When Jesus said, "I am the resurrection and the life" (John 11:25), how did his words and what he later accomplished through his death and resurrection change the game?

What ultimate hope do these words provide for us?

What implications do these words have for us in how we play the game today?

Bible Exploration (20 minutes)

1. Sometimes, as God's people play the game, they make a move that puts them in a square that has no way out. For example, when Moses led the Israelites to the shores of the Red Sea (Exodus 14), it looked like the last square. When Daniel defied the king's edict by praying to God and ended up in a pit of hungry lions, it looked like the last square (Daniel 6). When Jesus, the promised Messiah, was crucified and placed in a tomb, it looked like the last square. But often, when things seem impossible, the King has one more move and he acts in powerful ways on behalf of those who put their trust in him.

   a. During the last hours of Jesus' life, where was each roll of the dice leading? (See Matthew 27:11–14, 22–24, 27–31.)

   b. From a human perspective, how do we know Jesus had reached the last square? Were there any moves left? (See Matthew 27:35, 50, 57–60.)

c. What last move did the King make, and what impact did it have on the world of Jesus' day and on all humanity? (See Matthew 28:1 – 7.)

d. Because of what God accomplished, because the King had one more move, what is the hope of every person who has received Jesus as Lord and Savior? (See 1 Peter 1:3 – 5.)

What difference has this move had on you and on how you play the game?

2. While Jesus was on earth, he spoke about how to play the game for rewards that really matter. As you read the following Bible passages, notice not only the rewards God gives to

people who love and obey him, but the kinds of moves he rewards. (See Matthew 5:11 – 12; 6:5 – 6, 31 – 33; 10:42; Luke 6:20 – 23.)

a. What do these passages reveal about what God values?

b. In what ways do these passages cause you to rethink the value of the earthly trophies we often pursue in life?

3. John Ortberg wrote, "The trophy that matters is not on our shelves or résumés. It is the soul that we become. That is the crown that we will one day cast before God."

a. Which trophies of this life truly delighted Paul's heart? (See 1 Thessalonians 2:19 – 20.)

b. In a story Jesus told about the rewards servants receive from their master, what great trophy did Jesus say a faithful servant would receive? (See Matthew 25:21.)

c. How valuable to us are the trophies that don't sit on our shelves?

To what extent are they a joy we earnestly pursue as we make our moves through life?

Are they valuable enough to us that we will change our game strategy in order to pursue them? Why or why not?

4. Many people today play the game in denial of the last square. They arrange their lives so they don't have to think about death. They work too hard, are addicted to people's approval, and are obsessed with security. Although we cannot escape the reality that our earthly game will end, we still long for something more. Jesus, our Savior, "the resurrection and the life" (John 11:25), has provided that something more for us.

As you read the following passages that describe the hope of every person who has put his or her faith in Jesus, share together what that hope means to you — how it strengthens or encourages you, how it alters the way you play the game.

1 Corinthians 15:50–57

2 Corinthians 5:1

Philippians 3:20–21

1 Thessalonians 4:16 – 18

Titus 1:1 – 2

1 Peter 1:3 – 6

1 John 5:11

What really matters as the game comes to an end is, Who have I been playing for? What have I been doing about that which lasts forever? How do I live so that I'm prepared to die?
JOHN ORTBERG

DVD Wrap-up (3 minutes)

As you watch this final DVD clip, feel free to jot down notes or questions.

Personal Journey:
To Do Now (5 minutes)

Life has no rewind button, so John Ortberg reminds us that life's moments can be "remembered, celebrated, or regretted — but can never be retrieved." When we come face to face with this fact, it often gets our attention — at least for a moment. We often start thinking about how we could use our time and gifts more effectively. We begin considering how to place more of our energy and resources into areas that have eternal value. So, if you're interested in playing the game that really counts, and to play it without regrets, start by asking yourself the following questions.

1. In which of the following categories do I already have regrets—or at least am on my way to creating them?

   • I would have loved more deeply.
   • I would have laughed more often.
   • I would have given more generously.
   • I would have lived more boldly.

2. In light of my answers to question one, what changes do I need to make—now?

3. What matters most to me, what are the things and who are the people I hold most dear, and what gaps do I see between what I value and the way I spend my time?

Personal Journey: To Do on Your Own

In order to play the game by God's rules, and to avoid filling up your life with activities that don't really matter, it's important to read the Bible and learn more about God and his desires for your life. In *When the Game Is Over, It All Goes Back in the Box*, John Ortberg emphasized four priorities on which each of us must focus in order to pursue life in God's kingdom.

1. Take a look at what the Bible says about each of these priorities and how they relate to what Jesus said in Matthew 6:33: "Seek first [God's] kingdom and his righteousness, and all these things will be given to you as well."

God — the Overarching Priority
What do we need to do to help us remember God and know him better? (See Psalm 1:1 – 2; Mark 1:35.)

Loving People
What can we learn from Jesus about being deeply present with people — treasuring our families, friends, neighbors, coworkers; coming alongside people in need? (See Matthew 8:1 – 7; 9:27 – 30; 14:13 – 14; Luke 14:13; John 4:7 – 26.)

Living Out Our Calling
What advice did Paul give to Timothy (1 Timothy 4:14),
and how does this relate to our discovering how God wants
us to add value to the world?

Joy
Jesus demonstrated a well-recognized capacity for joy that
drew people to him. How important is it for us to be joy
sharers as we receive God's blessings? (See Psalm 5:11 – 12;
28:7; 95:1 – 3; John 15:9 – 11; Philippians 4:4.)

2. Life's minutes are ticking by. One day you will die and you
   can't take anything with you. How will you choose to live
   each day? Now would be a good time to examine your life
   commitments. With God's help, use the chart on page 106 to
   examine what you are doing (or not doing) that could lead to
   deep regret. Then roll the dice; it's your next move.

Types of life commitments	Commitments I have made	How my commitments affect the way I play the game	Changes in commitment I might make
Dramatic (choosing a college, changing jobs)			
Routine (volunteering, assumed responsibilities)			
Unspoken (learning, leisure, addictions)			
Spiritual (knowing God)			

Hope Beyond the Final Square

When your last earthly move is made and you walk into that final square, do you know what you will be walking into? Jesus not only died on the cross to pay the penalty for our sins, he overcame physical death in order to open the door for us to have a personal relationship with God that will last for eternity.

If you have any questions about how the King's last move affects your life and your hope for something beyond the final square, look up the following verses and write out what they reveal.

Bible verses	What they reveal about you, God, and eternal hope
Ephesians 2:8–9	
John 3:16	
Romans 3:23	
Romans 6:23	
Acts 4:11–12	

WILLOW
Willow Creek Association

Willow Creek Association
Vision, Training, Resources for Prevailing Churches

This resource was created to serve you and to help you build a local church that prevails. It is just one of many ministry tools that are part of the Willow Creek Resources® line, published by the Willow Creek Association together with Zondervan.

The Willow Creek Association (WCA) was created in 1992 to serve a rapidly growing number of churches from across the denominational spectrum that are committed to helping unchurched people become fully devoted followers of Christ. Membership in the WCA now numbers over 12,000 Member Churches worldwide from more than ninety denominations.

The Willow Creek Association links like-minded Christian leaders with each other and with strategic vision, training, and resources in order to help them build prevailing churches designed to reach their redemptive potential. Here are some of the ways the WCA does that.

- **The Leadership Summit** — a once a year, two-and-a-half-day conference to envision and equip Christians with leadership gifts and responsibilities. Presented live at Willow Creek as well as via satellite broadcast to over 130 locations across North America, this event is designed to increase the leadership effectiveness of pastors, ministry staff, volunteer church leaders, and Christians in the marketplace.

- **Ministry-Specific Conferences** — throughout each year the WCA hosts a variety of conferences and training events — both at Willow Creek's main campus and offsite, across the U.S., and around the world — targeting church leaders and volunteers in ministry-specific areas such as: small groups, preaching and teaching, the arts, children, students, volunteers, stewardship, etc.

- **Willow Creek Resources®** — provides churches with trusted and field-tested ministry resources in such areas as leadership, evangelism, spiritual formation, spiritual gifts, small groups, stewardship, student ministry, children's ministry, the use of the arts-drama, media, contemporary music — and more.

- **WCA Member Benefits** — includes substantial discounts to WCA training events, a 20 percent discount on all Willow Creek Resources®, *Defining Moments* monthly audio journal for leaders, quarterly *Willow* magazine, access to a Members-Only section on WillowNet, monthly communications, and more. Member Churches also receive special discounts and premier services through WCA's growing number of ministry partners — Select Service Providers — and save an average of $500 annually depending on the level of engagement.

For specific information about WCA conferences, resources, membership, and other ministry services contact:

Willow Creek Association
P.O. Box 3188, Barrington, IL 60011-3188
Phone: 847-570-9812, Fax: 847-765-5046
www.willowcreek.com

God Is Closer Than You Think

Six Sessions on Experiencing the Presence of God

John Ortberg with Stephen and Amanda Sorenson

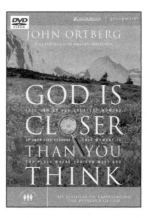

The story of the Bible is the story of God's desire to be with people. God is extending himself, stretching out to reach us, to fill our lives with his presence. Every moment of your life is like a page in a *Where's Waldo?* book. God is there, the Scriptures tell us — on every one of them. But the ease with which he may be found varies from one page to the next.

In this six-session ZondervanGroupware™ video curriculum, award-winning author John Ortberg serves as guide and interpretive leader for experiencing the presence of God in everyday life. With his engaging and humorous style, Ortberg transforms our view of God's presence from one that may seem hidden or distant to one that is closer than you think.

This six-session small group DVD (with a thirty-two-page leader's guide) features teaching from John Ortberg, and corresponds with the participant's guide, which is sold separately.

DVD 978-0-310-26637-2
Participant's Guide 978-0-310-26639-6

Pick up a copy today at your favorite bookstore!

If You Want to Walk on Water, You've Got to Get Out of the Boat

A Six Session Journey on Learning to Trust God

John Ortberg with Stephen and Amanda Sorenson

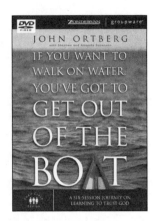

If You Want to Walk on Water, You've Got to Get Out of the Boat — Nearly 500,000 books sold

John Ortberg serves as guide and interpretive leader of six DVD small group sessions designed to help people learn to trust God more fully. Using testimonial interviews to illustrate his talks, Ortberg teaches participants the skills essential for "water-walking" in faith with God.

Small group Bible study will never be the same! With Zondervan-*Groupware*™ Small Group Editions, leaders have interactive DVDs that feature bestselling authors Philip Yancey and John Ortberg to teach a small group Bible study in their own homes. The DVD and 32-page leader's guide provide ease of facilitation for the small group leader. The participant's guide, available separately, provides a book for group members to follow along with the teaching and record responses to questions.

DVD 978-0-310-26180-3
Participant's Guide 978-0-310-25056-2

Pick up a copy today at your favorite bookstore!

The Life You've Always Wanted

Six Sessions on Spiritual Disciplines for Ordinary People

John Ortberg with Stephen and Amanda Sorenson

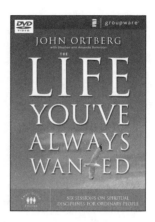

The Life You've Always Wanted — Over 300,000 books sold

In this six-session small group DVD curriculum, award-winning author John Ortberg offers modern perspectives on the ancient practice of spiritual disciplines — teaching participants the skills essential to "running the marathon" in the Christian life: slowing down, celebrating joy, practicing prayer, studying Scripture, and trusting God.

Small group Bible study will never be the same! With Zondervan-*Groupware*™ Small Group Editions, leaders have interactive DVDs that feature bestselling authors Philip Yancey and John Ortberg to teach a small group Bible study in their own homes. The DVD and 32-page leader's guide provide ease of facilitation for the group leader. The participant's guide, available separately, provides a book for group members to follow along with the teaching and record responses to questions.

DVD 978-0-310-26178-0
Participant's Guide 978-0-310-25588-8

Pick up a copy today at your favorite bookstore!

Faith and Doubt

John Ortberg, bestselling author of When the Game Is Over, It All Goes Back in the Box

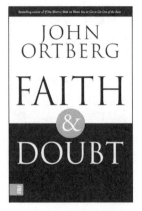

Is it possible to be a thinking person and be completely free of doubt? To believe without question? Author and pastor John Ortberg explores the nature of doubt and finds that it is not only common but inevitable, and in some ways necessary. How do we have unshaken faith in a God who seems to sit idle as an earthquake kills thousands? How can we firmly believe in a God that lets children perish in war or from disease or hunger? Calling on his own faith (and doubt) and the observations of philosophers and theologians, Ortberg grapples with when doubt and uncertainty are obstacles to faith, demonstrating what forms of doubt are damaging, and how we can open ourselves up to the gift of belief. He discusses the faith that hope delivers, a faith so strong and real that "I can let go and trust that Jesus will catch me."

Hardcover, Jacketed 978-0-310-25351-8